WITHDRAWN

W9-CAB-060

WITHDRAWN

Start TO Finish
Second Series

FROM Soil TO Garden

MARI SCHUH

LERNER PUBLICATIONS Minneapolis

Copyright © 2017 by Lerner Publishing Group, Inc.

All rights reserved. International copyright secured. No part of this book may be reproduced, stored in a retrieval system, or transmitted in any form or by any means—electronic, mechanical, photocopying, recording, or otherwise—without the prior written permission of Lerner Publishing Group, Inc., except for the inclusion of brief quotations in an acknowledged review.

Lerner Publications Company
A division of Lerner Publishing Group, Inc.
241 First Avenue North
Minneapolis, MN 55401 USA

For reading levels and more information, look up this title at www.lernerbooks.com.

Library of Congress Cataloging-in-Publication Data

Names: Schuh, Mari C., 1975– author.
Title: From soil to garden / by Mari Schuh.
Other titles: Start to finish (Minneapolis, Minn.). Second series.
Description: Minneapolis : Lerner Publications, [2016] | Series: Start to Finish, Second Series | Audience: Ages 5–9. | Audience: K to grade 3. | Includes bibliographical references and index.
Identifiers: LCCN 2015036530| ISBN 9781512409468 (lb : alk. paper) | ISBN 9781512413021 (pb : alk. paper) | ISBN 9781512410860 (eb pdf)
Subjects: LCSH: Gardens—Juvenile literature. | Gardening—Juvenile literature.
Classification: LCC SB457 .S375 2016 | DDC 635—dc23

LC record available at http://lccn.loc.gov/2015036530

Manufactured in the United States of America
1 – CG – 7/15/16

TABLE OF Contents

Gardens are beautiful. How do they grow?

First, gardeners find a space.

Gardeners put their gardens where plants will grow well. Many vegetables need to be in the sun for six or more hours a day. Gardeners also choose an area that will be easy to water.

Then they test the soil.

Testing the soil gives gardeners information about their soil. They find out if it has enough **nutrients** for their plants to grow well. They can improve the soil by adding **fertilizer** or **compost**.

Gardeners loosen the soil.

Gardeners dig into the ground with a **hoe** or pitchfork. They break up large chunks of soil and get rid of rocks and weeds. They rake the soil to make it even.

Next, gardeners buy seeds and plants.

There are many kinds of gardens. Gardeners can grow flowers, **herbs**, fruits, and vegetables. Sometimes gardeners plant seeds. They also start gardens with small plants called **seedlings**.

They plant their gardens.

Gardeners carefully plant seeds and seedlings where they will grow the best. Sometimes they put a fence around the garden to keep out rabbits and other animals that might eat the plants.

Then they water their gardens.

Gardeners water their gardens in the early morning or evening. Then plants can soak up the most water. First, gardeners check the soil to see if it is dry. Then they water the garden using watering cans, sprinklers, or **soaker hoses**.

Gardeners add mulch.

Many gardeners use mulch, such as straw or wood chips. They put a layer of mulch on top of the soil. Mulch **insulates** the soil and keeps it moist. It can also keep weeds out of the garden.

They pull weeds.

Weeds use up nutrients, sunlight, and water.
This can make it hard for other plants to grow.
Gardeners pull weeds often. They use tools, or
they pull weeds by hand.

Finally, the garden grows!

It is time to enjoy the garden. Gardeners carefully pick vegetables when they are ripe. The **fertile** soil helped them grow. Try planting your own garden. You will have fun watching it grow!

Glossary

compost: a mixture of rotted leaves, grass, vegetables, and other items that is used to improve soil

fertile: good for growing lots of plants

fertilizer: something added to soil to make plants grow better

herbs: plants that are used in cooking or for medicine

hoe: a tool with a flat blade and a long handle

insulates: stops heat or cold from coming in or going out

mulch: a covering of leaves, straw, sawdust, wood chips, or other material that is spread on the soil in a garden

nutrients: substances that plants need to stay healthy

seedlings: small, young plants

soaker hoses: hoses with many small holes that water drips out of. Soaker hoses are placed near plants so that water can slowly reach the plants' roots.

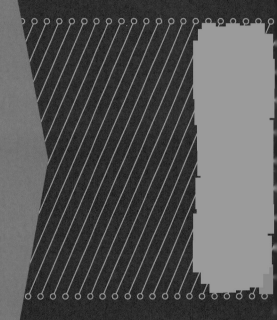

Further Information

Fretland VanVoorst, Jenny. *Gardens in Spring.* Minneapolis: Bullfrog Books, 2016. Read this book to learn how gardens grow in the spring.

Higgins, Nadia. *Experiment with a Plant's Living Environment.* Minneapolis: Lerner Publications, 2015. Discover how plants grow best by doing your own simple experiments.

Junior Master Gardener: Kids Zone
http://jmgkids.us/kids-zone
Visit this website to work on activities about plant growth, soil, and gardens.

Messner, Kate. *Up in the Garden and Down in the Dirt.* San Francisco: Chronicle Books, 2015. Learn about the animals and critters that live in and below gardens.

National Geographic Kids: Plant a Garden
http://kids.nationalgeographic.com/explore/nature/plant-a-garden/?ar_a=1
Check out this website for simple steps on how to start your own garden.

University of Illinois Extension: My First Garden
http://extension.illinois.edu/firstgarden
Learn gardening basics and how to plan your first flower and vegetable gardens.

Index

Photo Acknowledgments

The images in this book are used with the permission of:
© SeDmi/Shutterstock.com, p. 1; © Madlen/Shutterstock.com, p. 3; © DeepGreen/Shutterstock.com, p. 5; © Julija Sapic/Shutterstock.com, p. 7; © iStockphoto.com/Petegar, p. 9; © kreatorex/Shutterstock.com, p. 11; © stockphoto mania/Shutterstock.com, p. 13; © iStockphoto.com/fotokostic, p. 15; © Matthew Benoit/Shutterstock.com, p. 17; © iStockphoto.com/ Rich Legg, p. 19; © iStockphoto.com/Christopher Futcher, p. 21.

Front cover: © 135pixels/Shutterstock.com.

Main body text set in Arta Std Book 20/26.
Typeface provided by International Typeface Corp.

LERNER
e
SOURCE™

Expand learning beyond the printed book. Download free, complementary educational resources for this book from our website, www.lerneresource.com.